Date Ninja

75 Kick-Awesome Date Ideas

By:
Claire Wilson

Photography By:
Bekah Van Goor

Contents

Introduction:
Page 1

1. Dates so Cheap Even a College Ninja Could Afford Them:
Page 5

2. Dates for the Procrastinating Ninja:
Page 21

3. Double Dates That Will Win You Ninja Friends:
Page 35

4. Dates Only a Liberal Arts Major Would Think Of:
Page 55

Conclusion:
Page 68

Dedication

First, I want to thank my family and good friends (Sam and Alex) for editing. You made this book better.

And, this book would never have seen the light of Amazon if not for my husband. Thank you, Glenn, for all your encouragement, optimism, and making me write when I would rather watch Netflix. You are the best!

www.FireLeafPublishing.com

Copyright © 2014 Fire Leaf Publishing

ISBN-13: 978-1503394995

Want to get an email about future book releases from us?

Sign up here: http://eepurl.com/EPGsH

Introduction

My husband, Glenn, came home from work one day to find me sitting in the middle of the living room with my iHome.

"What's . . . up?" he asked.

"I have hidden paper hearts throughout the house. Each one has a favor I'll do for you if you find them," I said. "You have until the end of this song to find the hearts. Whatever you find, I'll do."

"What are you—"

"Go!" I said, pressing "Play" on my iPod. Glenn immediately dropped his work stuff, kicked off his shoes, and tore around the house, looking for paper hearts.

After a few minutes, the song ended, and Glenn had found five hearts.

"How many did I miss?" he asked.

"Only a couple," I said, pulling one from the ice cube tray, and another from the back of a picture frame.

"Well, that's cheap," he smiled. "That was really fun, though. What a way to come home from work." He looked through the hearts and cashed in the one for a "free massage."

After that, I started to create a lot more dates for us. I wasn't working at the time because of some health issues. Our limited budget forced me to get creative, but luckily, I had a lot of time on my hands. Now, after three years of marriage, I have quite the list of date ideas.

Some of you may be wondering about the title of this book. Perhaps some of you bought this book thinking, "Awesome, black is my favorite color" or "I want to learn how to go on a date without the other person knowing I'm there . . . like a ninja." First of all, I think that's officially called "stalking," and I don't endorse that. Second of all, I'm not a licensed ninja, so I can't train you to be invisible like the night. I just want people to be expert daters, and there's no rank higher than ninja. I mean, Batman is a ninja, so . . .

When my husband and I got married, we received a lot of advice on how to have a successful marriage. Some of it was very helpful (do finances together), and some of it seemed to be a no-brainer (don't have an affair). But, one big piece of advice that I received from my parents was how important it is to "keep dating." Having a date night every week or two, especially with young kids, keeps you connected with your spouse as a lover, instead of just becoming a tag team.

And if you have kids, the best thing you can do for them is to have a strong marriage. Keeping the romance alive and making time for yourselves will richly benefit them. I know it can be tough if you have a busy schedule or a tight budget, but I have compiled a list of easy and cheap dates anyone can do. I mean, my husband and I are both English majors, so we know how to have cheap dates!

If you're not married and reading this book, this is a great list of creative dates to do with your boyfriend/girlfriend. Don't be intimidated, there are a lot of fun things to do that will help you get to know each other and make memories. And, I highly recommend marriage. It's totally awesome.

Anyway, this is a book full of date ideas to help you, married or not, excel in the romance department. So good luck. And may you be invisible like the night (that's probably a ninja catchphrase, right?).

Dates so Cheap Even a College Ninja Could Afford Them

Glenn and I started dating our senior year in college. Back then, I was only working part-time as a cashier at a grocery store. A full-time job was at the back of my mind (because I woke up one night and realized that student loans were coming to get me). But at the time, as long as I had money for food, clothes, and Starbuck's Frappuccinos, I was pretty content.

Then, Glenn and I started dating. I wanted to buy him giant gifts and do grand romantic gestures. If I cut out my coffee habit, that would give me . . . $10 a week to work with. It wasn't quite enough to cover the dove ice sculpture I wanted to get Glenn, so I had to get creative.

I went to the dollar store and got a bag of army men. On the bottom, I numbered them 1-15. Then, on notecards, I wrote 15 things I admired about him. There was a park close to the campus (called "Wilson Park." How's that for foreshadowing?) where I hid the army men. I texted Glenn to meet me there. When he arrived, I told him the rules: every army man he finds correlates to a love note he'll get to read.

After half an hour, he had only found the six obvious ones. I decided to help him, but after thirty minutes, we were still only at ten. See, green army men are incredibly hard to find in green flower gardens, and I hadn't kept a list of where I hid them. Personally, I think the punk squirrels stole them, but that's a different paranoia.

I gave Glenn all the love notes anyway, and we sat in front of the fountain as Glenn read his notes by fountain light. It was really fun and romantic and had only cost me $1. I even had Frappuccino money left.

    I know, as a college kid, you feel like you can't have anything nice. Maybe some of you have decided not to date because you'd have to take out a student loan for a girlfriend/boyfriend. But whether you're single, dating, or married and on a tight budget, don't give up hope! In fact, I'd say it's more fun dating on a tight budget because it forces you to use your imagination. And in my experience, those tend to be the most memorable dates. Here are some examples to get you started:

1. Camouflage Compliments: Pick up a bag of toys, like army men, and number them on the bottom. Then, cut out strips of paper, and on each one write something you love or admire about the person. Next, label them with numbers corresponding to the army men. Hide the army men around the house or outside, and then have the other person search for them. When they find an army man, they can redeem it for the corresponding note.

2. Framed: With a camera or phone, each of you will take five pictures privately. Then, have them developed, and if you're brave, frame them! Each person will take a picture pertaining to these categories (make sure you're in them too!):

- Take a picture representing a fun nickname you have for the other person.
- Take a picture of the other person's favorite place.
- Take a picture that will be sure to make the other laugh.
- Take a picture of something you both find annoying.
- Take a picture of something that you both have fond memories of.

3. Prize Poker: On slips of paper, write various activities you would do for the other person. They can be things like "coffee date" or "homemade cheesecake." Price them from 5 cents to a dollar. Then, for a set time, play penny poker. Start with $1-2 a person. When time is up, use your winnings to purchase various activities the other person is offering.

4. Learn a New Love Language: If you've never read *The 5 Love Languages* by Gary Chapman, this is a very helpful date night idea. Its premise is that there are five main love languages: gifts, words of affirmation, touch, acts of service, and quality time. Though all are ways to show love, some are more meaningful to an individual than others. For instance, when my husband and I went through the book, we realized that we had opposite love languages!

Gifts were a 10 for me. So, I kept getting

Glenn little presents. And he felt fine about them, but gifts were a 1 for him. His 10 was touch, and touch was a 1 for me. Knowing that really helped us be intentional about expressing love in the language that is important to the other person. It really is like learning a new language! Check it out from the library and figure out your main love languages. There's also a free test you can do online at 5lovelanguages.com.

5. Favorite Fun: Each of you makes a list of your favorite things. For instance, I love superhero movies, dark chocolate, night walks, and berry picking. Then, for the next few date nights, take turns doing things from your favorites list.

6. Sweet and Sticky Notes: Each of you will get a post-it note pad and a pen. Throughout the week, write nice things about the other person on post-it notes and hide them places where the other will be sure to find them.

7. Extreme Makeover: Go to a furniture store and walk around. Talk about which pieces, if money were no object, you would buy to decorate your home. For instance, if I were fabulously wealthy, I would have the floor of every room covered with bean bags. Then, I would try to run around the house.

8. Love You to a T: Get some plain-colored shirts and fabric markers. Spend the evening decorating a t-shirt for the other person. For instance, on the back, write some of the funniest things your spouse/significant other has said.

9. Heart Hunt: Make 10-20 paper hearts and write various favors on them, such as: do dishes one night, 10 minute back rub, or homemade romantic dinner. Hide these around a room. When your spouse or significant other gets home, tell him/her that there are paper hearts hidden around the room, and he/she has a limited amount of time to find them all. Then, either set a timer for 3-5 minutes, or play a favorite song. When the time is up, they get to redeem whatever they have found.

10. Shoe-String Dates: Each of you gets to be in charge of a date night. Have a competition to see who can create the best date night with $5. For instance, Glenn once made a board game for me with note cards and dice.

11. Tradition!: For those who are married, create new family traditions. For instance, you could decide that on birthdays, you fix the birthday person breakfast in bed. Or every second weekend of each month you go tech-free (no computer, TV, or cell phone).

12. Brown Paper Packages Tied up in String: Over dinner or during a walk, find out each other's favorite things. Take turns asking what the other person's favorites are. Here are some questions to get you started:

- Who is your favorite cartoon character?

- What is your favorite state?
- Favorite flavor of ice cream?
- Favorite family tradition?
- Favorite mythical creature?
- Favorite famous person?
- Favorite time of day?
- Favorite way of traveling?
- Favorite food type?
- Favorite past time?

13. Stroll Down Memory Lane: Pack a car picnic and visit all the memorable spots in your relationship. For instance, first place you met, first place you kissed, place you went for your first date. Reminisce together at each spot.

14. MacGyver It: With just the items in your car, see who can create the most romantic gift for the other person. If you're messy like I am, you'll have a lot to work with. Right now, I have a chair cushion, artificial flowers, empty MacDonald's bag, and a coffee cup. Maybe I'll try a recycled bouquet.

15. Mosquito-Free Drive-in Movie: In your car, pack blankets, snacks, and something to watch movies on (laptop, phone, or tablet). Snuggle up and watch a movie with the windows up so that the bugs can't get you.

16. Thirty Days of Kisses: Each day, try out a different kiss:

- *Flavored kiss*- Either with flavored lip gloss or rubbing food on your lips (like chocolate or a popsicle), taste the sweetness of the kiss.
- *Eskimo kiss*- Rub noses back and forth with each other.

- *Spider-man kiss-* If you've never seen the movie, it's when Mary Jane kisses Spider-man while he's hanging upside down. You don't have to be suspended from a spider web to do it, though.
- *Cheek kiss-* Like it sounds, it's a kiss on the cheek.
- *Hand kiss-* Gently hold the person's hand in yours and kiss the back of the hand and fingers.
- *French kiss-* It's when you run away when someone tries to kiss you. Just kidding! I think we all know what this is.
- *Slick kiss-* With a generous amount of Chapstick or lip gloss on your lips, this kiss is pretty slippery.
- *Raspberry kiss-* Put your lips tight against their skin and blow until your lips vibrate.

- ***Butterfly kiss*-** Flutter your eyelashes against your partner's eyelashes.
- ***Spinning kiss*-** Before you kiss, spin around a couple of times, then try to kiss each other.
- ***Lady and the Tramp kiss*-** With a spaghetti noodle, Twizzler, etc., eat your way through until your lips meet.
- ***Earlobe kiss*-** Touch your lips to their ear.
- ***Underwater kiss*-** Hope you can hold your breath!
- ***Neck kiss*-** This'll give you goose bumps.
- ***Eyes wide open kiss*-** The habit is to close the eyes, but keep them open.
- ***Bubblegum kiss*-** Blow a bubble and pop it by kissing.
- ***Dip kiss*-** Just like in the old movies.
- ***Rain kiss*-** If the weather doesn't

cooperate, turn on the sprinkler.
- *Wing kiss*- Start at one hand, kiss across their arms, collar bone, down the other arm and hand.
- *Slow motion kiss*- Gooooo. Slooooow.
- *Interruption kiss*- Kiss while the other person is in the middle of a sentence.
- *Text kiss*- In texting lingo, it looks like this: :-*
- *Whipped Cream kiss*- Spread whipped cream on your lips and smooch it off.
- *Blow a kiss*- Catch it as floats to you.
- *Kiss on the nose*- Cute little peck on the end of the nose.
- *Polar plunge kiss*- Eat something cold like ice cream or an ice cube and then kiss.
- *Forehead kiss*- This is a really tender kiss.
- *World record kiss*- See how long you

can make it last.

- **_Fish kiss_**- Suck your cheeks together and then move your lips up and down.
- **_Ninja kiss_**- Sneak up on them and kiss.

Dates for the Procrastinating Ninja

I have many friends who plan date nights weeks in advance. They know where they're going to dinner, what time the movie starts, what kind of candy they'll buy, and which cup holders they'll use at the movie theater.

That is not us.

It's ironic, since we're both planners. But, Glenn's a long-term planner, which means that he has retirement figured out, but not this week's date night. And me? Well, I'm lazy. So, we're often trying to figure out a meaningful, romantic date last minute.

One of my favorite last-minute-dates was at the library. Glenn decided that we'd get candy bars and go through one of those "Choose Your

Own Adventure" books. The one we got was science fiction. It starts out where you're put in a stasis pod and wake up 100 years in the future. You have a choice to go back to Earth (which is now ruled by a ruthless dictator), Mars (which is a colony for the resistance), or Venus (it never did tell us what was cool about Venus, except that it was so hot that we'd probably die as soon as we landed). We decided to go to Mars first, where we were shortly eaten by Martian wolves. Then we went to Earth, where we were imprisoned as "resistance" and executed. I kid you not—we literally chose every bad ending in this book. We had to cheat to figure out how to get through the adventure alive. The key was to go to Venus and befriend the space butterflies (Doh! So obvious now . . .). After we cheated our way to our happy ending, we toasted our success with candy bars (though I had already stress-eaten half of mine after the fifth violent death in a row. This is a children's book??).

Glenn and I still laugh about it, and it was all planned on a fancy. There's a lot you can do on a time crunch. Try these out:

17. Lock Box Love Letter: Sit together and compose a love letter for the other person. Then lock the letters away and open them in a year.

18. Role Models: During dinner, a walk, or some other low-key activity, take turns describing qualities you'd like to have in your relationship and who in your life is a good model of that quality. For instance, I want to collaboratively write something with my husband, like my parents do. Or be really generous like our friends, Matt and Stephie.

19. True Blind Date: Have a romantic dinner at home. Once everything is on the table, blindfold yourselves and eat your meal without peeking. Now you can truly have a blind date!

20. The Pinocchio Game: Play 2 Truths and a Lie. Trust me, even though you think you know your spouse/intimate other inside out, this always brings up new things that'll surprise you! For instance:

> **1.** For a summer job, I juggled at a Renaissance Faire.
> **2.** When I got my wisdom teeth out, I hugged my doctor and thanked him for the drugs.
> **3.** When my brother was younger, I

convinced him to trade me his dimes for my nickels. I told him that since nickels were bigger, they were worth more.

Know which one is the lie? Number 2 . . . as much as I wish number 3 weren't true. I was a schemer as a child. Sorry lil' brother!

21. Jar of Thankfulness: Get two mason jars or bowls and slips of paper. Each of you then writes seven things you're thankful for about the other person on the slips of paper. Fold them up and put them in the jar. Swap jars and read a note a day. For instance, I'm thankful that:

    1. My husband is so funny.

    2. He buys me fried chicken when I'm feeling sad.

    3. He's really generous with his money.

4. He gets me a "get well" kit when I have a cold (orange juice, tea, NyQuil, and a Redbox movie).

5. He compliments every meal I cook.

6. He's a gentle soul.

7. He gets up at 2AM when I have a headache to rub my neck.

22. Go Back to Your Roots: Go to an ancestry website and trace your family trees. See who has the most exciting ancestor—that person wins a kiss!

23. Dinner Improv: Make a romantic meal at home . . . using only the stuff you have in the cupboard. No shopping beforehand!

24. Music Awards: With a video camera or with your phone, film a kick-awesome music video of the other person's favorite song. If you're brave, post it on Youtube.

25. Back to School: Has it been awhile since you've been to school? Have a school night and listen to some educational podcasts. Khan Academy is a great resource for this. Cuddle up on the couch, make a snack, and learn about the Renaissance or entrepreneurship. Afterwards, discuss what you found interesting, what you disagreed with, and what you learned.

26. Survive an Adventure: Go to the youth section in the library and checkout one of those "Choose Your Own Adventure" books. Try to make it to the end without dying!

27. Face Your Fears: Make a list of things you're afraid of (spiders, clowns, public speaking). Each of you picks one fear and faces them on this date. I have a thing with heights, so Glenn and I went on a gondola ride. I had lockjaw by the end of it, but I did it.

28. Habit Forming: Experts say it takes 30 days to form a new habit. Each of you should write down 12 new habits you want to learn, and then learn one each month. Keep each other accountable, and at the end of the month, reward yourselves with a treat!

29. A Date Idea with Personality: Take the Myers-Briggs or any other mainstream personality test. It's a great way to get to know yourself and each other. Most of my life, I've had extrovert envy. They're so natural around people and social events. My idea of a social event is a book club where we read the same book . . . in separate houses . . . and never talk about it. But, the Myers-Briggs explains introvert/extrovert as an indicator of how you get your energy. My brother, the extrovert, needs to be around people to reenergize. But I get drained easily at social events and need alone time to recharge. I can always learn to be more outgoing, but it's good to know that I need to put aside time alone to recharge. Personality tests are great tools for articulating personal characteristics to someone.

30. LOST: Hop in the car and get lost. Then, try to find your way back home. Make sure you have a GPS or a map as a backup!

31. Genie Night: For a night, do whatever the other person wishes. You can limit it to 3 wishes if you're scared.

32. World Record Dinner: Pick a meal you would like to eat and see how fast you can make it. Make it again in the next few weeks and see if you can beat your record.

33. High-Stakes People Watching: Bet on people in public (discreetly, so that they don't hear you). For instance, go to a Walmart self-checkout and bet on how long it will take for the person ahead of you to check out. Or, pick someone in front of you at the movie theater and bet which movie they're going to see.

34. Secret Busters: Take a deck of 52 cards and pick four of the cards. Redraw if there are any duplicates. These cards are the "secret buster" cards. Now, shuffle the cards and spread them out on the table face down. Each of you takes a turn drawing a card. If it's one of the four "secret busters," you have to tell something the other person doesn't know. For more flair, you can also add additional penalties, like the person has to take a shot of pickle juice or put an ice cube down his or her shirt.

35. Flash Memory: Each person writes their answers to the following questions. Then, switch answers. You have 1 minute to memorize the other person's responses. After a minute, switch back and quiz each other on the answers. Whoever gets the most right wins!

- Who is your favorite superhero?
- What was the make and model of your first car?

- If you could fight one celebrity and win, who would it be?
- What's the scariest movie you've ever seen?
- What's your shoe size?
- What's your favorite type of cereal?
- Mild, Medium, or Hot salsa?
- Favorite musical band?
- Who is the most famous person you've met?
- As a kid, how much money did you get from the Tooth Fairy per tooth?
- What's your favorite video game?
- Which TV show do you connect with the most?
- If you could be any book character, who would you be?
- If you had to get a tattoo, where would you put it and what would it be of?
- How many cavities do you have?

- Favorite flavor of ice cream?
- Least favorite animal?
- What's something you find boring?
- Favorite type of shampoo?
- If you could fill a pool with any substance other than water and go swimming in it, what would it be?

DOUBLE DATES THAT WILL WIN YOU NINJA FRIENDS

You know those fancy wine tastings people do? Well, wine's expensive, so we did an Oreo tasting. With Mozart music in the background, I covered the table with a cream-colored tablecloth. Each setting had a crystal wine glass and a red dessert plate. In the middle of the table, I set up my silver candleholder and lit the four taper candles. I even looked on Youtube to learn how to fold the cloth napkins into flowers (which took me an hour and a half, even with my college education. I'm convinced there's an element of magic to it.).

Once our guests arrived, I poured everyone

milk from the decanter. Then, the tasting began. The first taster was blindfolded and given the first Oreo. We had seven different flavors, and we had the challenge of guessing each one correctly. The two tricky ones were birthday cake and golden—they tasted almost identical.

When it came to Glenn's turn . . . I couldn't resist. I combined different Oreos together to trick him. The first was caramel apple and mint. Glenn took a bite and then made a gagging sound.

"Gross," Glenn said. "This must be pumpkin spice."

Our friend, Ryan, covered his mouth to stifle his laughter. I recorded Glenn's answer, and then I handed him a glass of milk to cleanse his pallet. He swished it around his mouth, swallowed, and then held out his hand for the next one. I gave him a caramel apple Oreo. Glenn nibbled it and then said, "Caramel apple."

I wrote down his answer and gave him milk.

Then I handed him another caramel apple Oreo. Glenn took a bite, and with a full mouth said,

"Oh, this is definitely berry." Again, our friend Ryan turned around to cover his laughing. By the end, Glenn had only gotten three flavors right . . . which is amazing considering how much I tinkered with the cookies.

"Cheater!" Glenn said when he saw the spliced cookies on his plate. Everyone started laughing. "I'll need all kinds of counseling after this," he said over us. "Oreos will never be the same."

Double or triple dates are awesome, and you can really have some fun times. It's also a great way to make friends or get to know the ones you already have even better. Check these out:

36. Toy Poker: Have a poker night with other couples, but instead of playing with poker chips, play with toys from the dollar store. (You can assign values to each toy. I.E. army men are worth 5 cents, toy cars are 10 cents, bouncy balls are worth 20 cents, etc.). You decide what the winner gets.

37. Private Art Exhibit: Art exhibits are fun, but creating your own exclusive exhibit is even better. Each person creates 2 pieces of art, displays them, and then acts as a tour guide for the other people—explaining the history, meaning, and value of each piece.

38. Dessert Dinner: On a hot day during the summer, have an ice cream dinner. Buy ice cream, toppings, and enjoy! But, you better eat all of your ice cream, or you don't get any broccoli for dessert.

39. Triathlon Double Date: Devise three categories to compete in. These could be board games, root beer chugging contest, trivia, etc. If you're really hardcore, require each team to wear matching uniforms. Losing couple must buy dessert.

40. Secret Egg Hunt: This one is a double date, though the other couple isn't aware the game is going on. Have dinner at another couple's house. Throughout the evening, you and your spouse/intimate other will try to hide Easter eggs filled with candy in their house. First one to get caught loses. And it will really confuse your friends later!

41. White Elephant Date Exchange: Ever done a white elephant gift exchange at Christmas? This is a white elephant *date* exchange. Each person will put items in a box for a date night and wrap it. Going in a circle, first person picks a box. The next person can choose to steal or pick one out of the center. Each person only gets to steal once. As soon as everyone has a box, open them up. They'll be future dates you can do with your spouse/romantic other at a later date! Ideas for boxes:

- Popcorn, a DVD, and baby oil (for massages during the movie).

- Fake mustaches, hats, and a secret mission outlined on a note card.
- Treasure map and an envelope of hints where you hid a treasure (like wine or a gift card) for the other couple to find.
- Have a note card with five random acts of kindness the couple has to do on their date. For instance: putting money in a parking meter, covering the bill for the people behind you in the drive thru, bringing back carts at the back of the Walmart parking lot, or buying a candy bar for the cashier at a store.
- Include Candyland and a bag of sour candy. The new Candyland has a spinner, so include the rule that whoever spins a certain color (like blue) has to eat a sour candy. If you have the old school version, it's whenever someone draws a certain color.

42. Sensational Date: Construct a double date with activities that use all of the five senses. For instance: for taste, you could sample candy. For smell, you could have an air freshener spray fight. For touch, you could eat pudding with your hands. For sight, you could set off fireworks. And for hearing, you could explore new music on Pandora or Spotify.

43. G Night: You know how Sesame Street used to have a "letter of the day"? Maybe they still do, I haven't seen the show since I was a kid (and it's frowned upon to watch kid shows as an adult). Have a date night that is dedicated to the letter "G."

- Gyros for dinner.
- Make gingerbread men together and have them for dessert.
- Watch Godzilla.

- Buy a goldfish and name him Gilbert.
- See how many gumballs you can chew.

44. Olympic Course: Create a backyard obstacle course. Time each person as they go through it, and the fastest person gets a prize. Possible obstacles:

- Ride a kid's tricycle to the back of the house.
- Find 5 dimes hidden in a bucket of sand (the sand is not allowed to leave the bucket).
- Chug a can of soda and then spin around 10 times.
- Melt an ice cube.
- Hop on one foot across the yard.
- Put on an old suit over your clothes.
- Fill a water balloon. Then, put it between your knees and walk a certain

distance without dropping or breaking the balloon. If you do, you have to go back, fill up a new balloon, and start over.

• Eat an anchovy.

• Take the suit off.

• Create a series of tunnels from boxes which you must crawl through.

45. Russian Roulette Date: Disclaimer: This one is only for the brave (or Russian). Everyone will write down a date idea on a piece of paper. If you have four people, three people will each write a good date idea, and one person will write down a terrible date idea. If you have six people, two people will write down terrible dates, and so on. Put each idea in a separate, identical envelope. Then, mix up the envelopes and pick one. Whatever it is, you have to do it! Here are some ideas for terrible dates:

- Watching the movie *The Dark Crystal* and eating black licorice. Seriously, *The Dark Crystal* is the creepiest kid's puppet movie I've ever seen.
- Going out to eat at the strangest restaurant you know.
- Order cement mixer shots at a restaurant or bar. That's when you hold a shot of Bailey's Irish Cream in your mouth and then take a sip of lime juice. The juice causes the Bailey's to curdle in your mouth. So gross.
- Go to a baseball game, observe the majority of fans around you, and then cheer for the opposite team.
- Have an outdoor picnic at night or in the winter.

46. Formal Oreo Tasting: Set up for a formal dessert night: nice tablecloth, candles, wine glasses, and all the guests must dress up. Then, serve gourmet Oreo flavors (mint, cookie dough, berry, etc.) on plates with wineglasses filled with milk for dunking. If you want a challenge, blindfold people and have them guess each flavor. The person who gets the most right wins.

47. Garage Sale Scavenger Hunt: Each couple has one hour to get as many of the following as possible:

- A Danielle Steel novel
- A baby's onesie with a monkey on it
- A superhero action figure
- The largest size of high heels you can find (whoever finds the biggest heels wins)
- A movie produced before 1990 (whoever finds the oldest movie wins)
- A sweater with cats on it
- Something definitely from the 70's
- Ice cube trays
- Red nail polish
- A gaudy piece of jewelry

48. Date with a lot of Dough: Ever done a wine tasting? Yeah, wine's too expensive. Go around to different bakeries and do a donut tasting.

49. Relay Dinner Race: You might want to do this one outside or in a place easy to clean up. Set up various stations like: drink table, salad table, main course table, and dessert table. One person from each couple runs to the first table and drinks the beverage as fast as they can. Then they run back and tag in their partner who goes to the next table and downs the salad. The first couple to complete the dinner relay race wins.

50. Landmark Treasure Hunt: Get a bag of fake gold coins or wrapped candy and give each couple five of them. Then, each couple will take five pictures of recognizable and accessible landmarks, hiding a coin somewhere close by. Next, meet up again and email or text the pictures to the other couple. After you've exchanged pictures, compete against the other couple to find the places in the pictures and collect all five coins!

51. Cage Fight: It's a Nicholas Cage night! Everyone bring a movie Cage is in and dress up as that character. Vote on the best Nicholas Cage movie, and watch it (and act like Cage the rest of the night).

52. I'd Rather Be Eating Bacon: Besides chocolate, bacon is the best food in the world. Have a night dedicated to bacon's goodness. Cook up a pan or two of bacon, and then see who can bring the craziest bacon product. For instance, did you know there is bacon-flavored toothpaste? How about bacon vodka? BACON SHAVING CREAM?? Make sure you try the products each person brings.

53. Good Cause: Donate the time and money you would have spent on a date to a local charity or non-profit. You could all walk dogs together, serve at a soup kitchen, or sort donations. It really helps the organization out, and it feels good to give back.

54. The "Newlywed Game": How well do you know your spouse/date? This is a fun game to play with other couples. Give each person a piece of paper and a pen. As you read each question, have both people write their answers down, and then see if they match. Go through this questionnaire and see which couple gets most right.

For Men
- If your wife/girlfriend could get rid of one thing of yours, what would it be?
- What food does your wife/girlfriend

crave the most?
- Say the house was on fire. Every person and pet is out safe, and there is time to save one thing. What one thing would your wife/girlfriend save?
- What would your wife/girlfriend say is the strangest gift you've ever gotten her?
- What profession did your wife/girlfriend want to be when she was little?
- Out of all the people in her family, who is she closest to?
- If she had a day to herself, what would she do?
- How would she finish this sentence? "The most important quality in a relationship is _____."
- What is her favorite Disney movie?
- If she had to pick a candy bar to represent your relationship, what would it be?

For Women
- What is something your husband/boyfriend thinks you have too much of?
- When you first met, what was the first thing your husband/boyfriend noticed about you?
- What is his favorite meal?
- What would he say is the last thing you argued about?
- What would he say is his greatest strength?
- What one animal can he not stand?
- What video game is most nostalgic for him?
- Would he rather be the star of a Western, Action Flick, Mystery, or Comedy movie?
- If he could build anything with his bare hands, what would he build?

- How would he finish this sentence? "An ideal wife is one who _____."

55. Classic Game Night: You can get many of these board games cheap at Walmart or Target if you don't already own them. These include: Go-Fish, Candyland, Hi Ho Cherrio, Chutes and Ladders, etc. Losers of the game must do something childish like:

- Chase a squirrel up a tree.
- Prank call someone.
- Ding-dong ditch a neighbor.
- Eat dinner with your hands.
- Stand on your head on the couch for a solid minute.
- Make a picture to hang on the fridge.

56. Glow in the Dark Date: Get a different color of glow sticks for each team, buying 10 of each color. Divide them up between each couple, and when it gets dark, activate them. Each couple will hide the opposing team's glow sticks in sneaky (but fair) places. Then, whichever couple finds all of their team's glow sticks first wins.

Dates Only a Liberal Arts Major Would Think Of

One of our funniest dates was when we made comic books for each other. First, we illustrated the comic panels. We then switched, and the other person filled in all the narration and dialogue bubbles. That's where it got funny. I clearly illustrated a superhero fighting back a robot invasion, but Glenn turned it into a romance. The robots were trying to find their soul mates, and the evil superhero was trying to stop them.

We had our stuff spread out on the café table when our poetry professor walked by. He's had several poetry books published, so he's a pretty big deal. Well, he sees us hunched over, scribbling with crayons, and asks what we're doing. We sheepishly reply,

"Making comics."

"Oh," he said, after a pause. "Well, I'm glad you're putting your education to good use." Then he walked away like a disappointed father. We hid the crayons after that.

Below are some date ideas that are out of the ordinary, which I think you'll enjoy. A little known fact: we liberal arts types are incredibly romantic. We know how to do more than just make coffee.

57. Comic Timing: Get out the colored pencils and paper—you'll be making your own comics. First, each of you will draw your comic without dialogue or captions. Once you're done illustrating, switch comics. The other person will be putting in the dialogue and captions to your comics. Once you're done, read them together.

58. The Alphabet Date: This one might take several weeks to complete. Working your way through the alphabet, go to places that start with each letter. For instance, one night you might go to an apple orchard or aquarium, the next night you might go to a bowling alley or bakery. Work your way to 'Z'!

59. For the Inner Writers: Go to the library to create writing prompts for each other! First, gather these samples that the other person will use to create their short story:

- Take a short opening line from a book. This will be the title of their story.
- Pick three characters from well-known books. These will be the main characters in their story.
- Take the ending line from a book. This will be the opening line of their story.
- Take a title of a movie. That title will be a "catch-phrase" the other must incorporate into their story.
- After collecting the four above, give

them to the other person. Sit down with notebooks and write a short story! (I find it helpful to have a time-limit, say, half an hour to an hour. Otherwise, you could be there all night.)

60. Thrifty Outfitters: Go to a discount store like Goodwill. Buy an outfit the other person will have to wear to dinner.

61. Machine Dinner: Get a roll of quarters and drive around town to different vending machines. Buy dinner from the machines.

62. Department Store Challenge: Go to a friendly store like Hollister or Best Buy. With a timer, see how long it takes each person to touch the back of the store and return to the car. The clincher: you have to make it through without a store employee asking if "you're finding everything okay" or greeting you. Winner gets a chicken dinner, or whatever you want.

63. Dollar Store Date: This is like a mini Christmas. Go to a dollar store together and buy items for each other that fit this list.

- Get something that will make the other person laugh.
- Get something that reminds you of an inside joke you share.
- Get something that reminds you of your childhood.
- Get something that reminds you of the other person.
- Get something for the other person to use as a utensil at dinner that night. Pick something funny (like a back-scratcher) and not mean (like thumbtacks).

64. Jenga, with a Twist: If you don't have a Jenga set, buy one. With permanent markers or really good pens, write actions a person has to do (I.E. run around the house, play the rest of the game with your finger on your nose, or you have to sing everything you say for the next ten minutes). Construct the Jenga tower, and every time you pull out a block, you must do what's written on it!

65. Buzz Word: Before you go out to dinner, buy a bag of chocolates. Each of you gets three chocolates to hang onto for the night. Then pick one "forbidden" word, a word you're not allowed to say for the night. It could be things like "dinner," "please," "love," etc. If you accidentally say the word and the other person calls you out, you must relinquish one of your chocolates to him or her. Winner is the one with all the chocolates at the end of the evening.

66. Facebook Zombie Apocalypse: For the evening, update your statuses like you're documenting a zombie apocalypse in progress. Bonus points for pictures. Then, sit back and read the comments.

67. Kid Night: Spend an evening as kids. Wear PJ's, have Lucky Charms for dinner, and watch an animated movie. Get it done before nine, though; that's bedtime.

68. Create a Holiday: Here are some unique holiday ideas. Make sure you celebrate whatever holiday you create each year.

- **Time Lord Day-** Even if you aren't a Dr. Who fan, you can enjoy Time Lord Day. Pick a time of day in hour increments (10-11AM, 12-1PM, etc.). Do something fun during that hour. Then, twelve hours later, repeat that same hour as close as you can. For instance, if you had pancakes at Perkins during your Time Lord hour (9-10AM), when it's 9PM, go to Perkins and get the same kind of pancakes.
- **Darth Vader's Birthday-** To my knowledge, no one knows when Vader's birthday is, so you get to choose! Make a Death Star cake, lightsaber party favors, and take pictures of you death-

choking someone.

- **Green Day**- You have to wear only the color green and can only eat green things this day.
- **Talk Like a Communist Day**- You know "Talk Like a Pirate Day?" Well, this day is dedicated to talking like a communist. What does that sound like? I'm glad you asked! Continually bring up the evils of materialism in conversation, and insult people by calling them "bourgeoisie." Also, randomly take people's stuff, explaining that you're redistributing wealth.

69. Off-Season Christmas: Have a summer Christmas. Play Christmas carols, hang mistletoe, exchange gifts, and snuggle up to *It's a Wonderful Life*. The hardest part will be finding eggnog.

70. Night of Firsts: There's a first for everything—do new things for the first time. For instance, I've never had vermouth, I've never seen *Terminator*, I've never eaten a veggie burger, and I've never gone to an outdoor concert. Make a date night of it!

71. Midnight Snack: Have a midnight snack together. This is convenient because you don't have to hire a babysitter!

72. Movie Words: Pick a movie you've never seen before. Beforehand, you each pick a word you think will be said a lot throughout the movie. Articles (the, a, etc.), conjunctions (and, but, etc.), and other cheating short words like that don't count. Challenge yourself! Keep track how many times your word is said during the movie. Then, whoever wins gets the agreed upon prize (foot rub, ice cream, etc.).

73. Where in the World: Where in the world is your date? Plan a date, but don't tell them where it is. Once you're there, text them "hotter or colder" as they guess where you are.

74. Dream List: Each of you make a list of 15 important qualities you want in a spouse. After you're done, pick the top five most important ones. Talk about them.

75. Secret Agent Date: Give your date a top secret envelope of missions to complete and hints to where they should meet you that night. For instance:

- **Mission #1-** Go to the grocery store and pick me up a sweet surprise.
- **Mission #2-** Pick a movie that was directed by Christopher Nolan.
- **Mission #3-** Dress up in a disguise.
- **Mission #4-** Come find me at 7PM. I'll be at the corner of two presidents' names. Call me if you get lost (the secret code is the name of my favorite candy bar).

Conclusion

My uncle once told me that if I had money to spend, I should spend it on experiences rather than stuff. He's travelled all over the world, and he said that memories always last longer than things.

I was pondering how to conclude this book—the big finale of why dating is so important. I didn't think you'd appreciate me saying, "Because I said so."

But, I want to draw on my uncle's wisdom. Dating is so important because you're building experiences and memories together. Marriage can be hard. When you're going through those rocky times with your spouse and think at the back of your mind, "Why did I marry this person?" I don't want you to come up blank.

During the hard times, I remember how Glenn

sent me on a treasure hunt for my birthday and buried my present in the backyard. It was a digital camera which he wrapped in a plastic bag before burying it. But unexpectedly, it started to rain, so Glenn was rushing me through the clues because he didn't want the camera to get wet. I started to dig in the wrong place when the rain erupted. Glenn took the shovel and said, "No, dig here!" He was on all fours, frantically digging with his fingers for the camera. It was the funniest thing.

    I remember how he made me his own "Choose Your Own Adventure" book, with all my favorite characters (Spider-man, Dr. Who, Sherlock, and Jack Sparrow). In one section, I was on a sinking boat with Jack Sparrow, and I had to choose whether to ride the sharks to shore or get the sharks drunk with the rum we had onboard (riding the sharks was the best option).

    I remember the love notes, the night walks, the couch cuddles, and countless other romantic things. It's the sweet memories that get me through the hard times and remind me why I married Glenn. But what memories will you have if you don't make them?

So, I hope this book helps you to make some beautiful memories. Those are the things that last.

Now that you're trained to date like a ninja, keep this momentum going and use your ninja skills to make your own creative date nights. Keep making new memories!

And, may you be invisible like the night.

www.FireLeafPublishing.com

Want to get an email about future book releases from us?

Sign up here: http://eepurl.com/EPGsH

Copyright © 2014 Fire Leaf Publishing

All rights reserved. No part of this publication may be reproduced, distributed, or transmitted in any form or by any means, including photocopying, recording, or other electronic or mechanical methods, without the prior written permission of the publisher, except in the case of brief quotations embodied in critical reviews and certain other noncommercial uses permitted by copyright law.

The writer of this book holds no liability for any potential injuries incurred while attempting any of its content.

Made in the USA
Coppell, TX
21 December 2019